American Sonnets
for My Past and Future
Assassin

American Sonnets for My Past and Future Assassin

TERRANCE HAYES

PENGUIN POETS

PENGUIN BOOKS

An imprint of Penguin Random House LLC
375 Hudson Street
New York, New York 10014
penguin.com

LIBRARY OF CONGRESS CATALOGING-IN-PUBLICATION DATA
Hayes, Terrance, author.
American sonnets for my past and future assassin / Terrance Hayes.
New York, New York : Penguin Books, 2018. | Series: Penguin poets
Identifiers: LCCN 2017057838|
ISBN 9780143133186 (paperback) |
ISBN 9780525504962 (ebook)
BISAC: POETRY / American / General. | POETRY / American / African
American.
LCC PS3558.A8378 A6 2018 | DDC 811/.54—dc23
LC record available at https://lccn.loc.gov/2017057838

Printed in the United States of America

3 5 7 9 10 8 6 4 2

Set in Adobe Garamond Pro   •   Designed by Catherine Leonardo

CONTENTS

bring me
to where
my blood runs

WANDA COLEMAN

American Sonnets
for My Past and Future
Assassin

AMERICAN SONNET FOR MY PAST AND FUTURE ASSASSIN

The black poet would love to say his century began
With Hughes or God forbid, Wheatley, but actually
It began with all the poetry weirdos & worriers, warriors,
Poetry whiners & winos falling from ship bows, sunset
Bridges & windows. In a second I'll tell you how little
Writing rescues. My hunch is that Sylvia Plath was not
Especially fun company. A drama queen, thin-skinned,
And skittery, she thought her poems were ordinary.
What do you call a visionary who does not recognize
Her vision? Orpheus was alone when he invented writing.
His manic drawing became a kind of writing when he sent
His beloved a sketch of an eye with an X struck through it.
He meant *I am blind without you*. She thought he meant
I never want to see you again. It is possible he meant that, too.

AMERICAN SONNET FOR MY PAST AND FUTURE ASSASSIN

Inside me is a black-eyed animal
Bracing in a small stall. As if a bird
Could grow without breaking its shell.
As if the clatter of a thousand black
Birds whipping in a storm could be held
In a shell. Inside me is a huge black
Bull balled small enough to fit inside
The bead of a nipple ring. I mean to leave
A record of my raptures. I was raised
By a beautiful man. I loved his grasp of time.
My mother shaped my grasp of space.
Would you rather spend the rest of eternity
With your wild wings bewildering a cage or
With your four good feet stuck in a plot of dirt?

AMERICAN SONNET FOR MY PAST AND FUTURE ASSASSIN

But there never was a black male hysteria
Because a fret of white men drove you crazy
Or a clutch of goons drove you through Money,
Stole your money, paid you money, stole it again.
There was a black male review for ladies night
At the nightclub. There was a black male review
By suits in the offices, the courts & waiting rooms.
There was a black male review in the weight rooms
Where coaches licked their whistles. Reviews,
Once-overs, half-studies, misreads & night
Mares looped the news. Your jolts & tears gained
Rubberneckers, eyeballers & bawlers in Money,
Mississippi. The stares you got were crazy,
It's true. But there never was a black male hysteria.

AMERICAN SONNET FOR MY PAST AND FUTURE ASSASSIN

Why are you bugging me you stank minuscule husk
Of musk, muster & deliberation crawling over reasons
And possessions I have & have not touched?
Should I fail in my insecticide, I pray for a black boy
Who lifts you to a flame with bedeviled tweezers
Until mercy rises & disappears. You are the size
Of a stuttering drop of liquid—milk, machine oil
Semen, blood. Yes, you funky stud, you are the jewel
In the knob of an elegant butt plug, snug between
Pleasure & disgust. You are the scent of rot at the heart
Of love-making. The meat inside your exoskeleton
Is as tender as Jesus. Neruda wrote of "a nipple
Perfuming the earth." Yes, you are an odor, an almost
Imperceptible ode to death, a lousy, stinking stinkbug.

AMERICAN SONNET FOR MY PAST AND FUTURE ASSASSIN

Probably twilight makes blackness dangerous
Darkness. Probably all my encounters
Are existential jambalaya. Which is to say,
A nigga can survive. Something happened
In Sanford, something happened in Ferguson
And Brooklyn & Charleston, something happened
In Chicago & Cleveland & Baltimore & happens
Almost everywhere in this country every day.
Probably someone is prey in all of our encounters.
You won't admit it. The names alive are like the names
In graves. Probably twilight makes blackness
Darkness. And a gate. Probably the dark blue skin
Of a black man matches the dark blue skin
Of his son the way one twilight matches another.

Are you not the color of this country's current threat
Advisory? And of pompoms at a school whose mascot
Is the clementine? Color of the quartered cantaloupe
Beside the tiers of easily bruised bananas cowering
In towers of yellow skin? And of Caligula's copper-toned
Jabber-jaw jammed with grapes shaped like the eyeballs
Of blind people? Light as a featherweight monarch,
Viceroy, goldfish. Pomp & pumpkin pompadour,
Are you not a flame of hollow *Hellos* & *Hell Nos*,
A wild, tattered spirit versus what? Enemy to Foe of
Those Opposed to Upholding the Laws Against What?
I know your shade. You are the color of a sucker punch,
The mix of flag blood & surprise blurring the eyes, a flare
Of confusion, a contusion before it swells & darkens.

AMERICAN SONNET FOR MY PAST AND FUTURE ASSASSIN

I lock you in an American sonnet that is part prison,
Part panic closet, a little room in a house set aflame.
I lock you in a form that is part music box, part meat
Grinder to separate the song of the bird from the bone.
I lock your persona in a dream-inducing sleeper hold
While your better selves watch from the bleachers.
I make you both gym & crow here. As the crow
You undergo a beautiful catharsis trapped one night
In the shadows of the gym. As the gym, the feel of crow-
Shit dropping to your floors is not unlike the stars
Falling from the pep rally posters on your walls.
I make you a box of darkness with a bird in its heart.
Voltas of acoustics, instinct & metaphor. It is not enough
To love you. It is not enough to want you destroyed.

AMERICAN SONNET FOR MY PAST AND FUTURE ASSASSIN

I pour a pinch of serious poison for you
James Earl Ray Dylann Roof I pour a punch of piss
For you George Zimmerman John Wilkes Booth
Robert Chambliss Thomas Edwin Blanton Jr
Bobby Frank Cherry Herman Frank Cash your name
Is a gate opening upon another gate I pour a punch
Of perils I pour a bunch of punches all over you
I pour unmerciful panic into your river I damn you
With the opposite of prayer Byron De La Beckwith
Roy Bryant J. W. Milam Edgar Ray Killen Assassins
Love trumps power or blood to trump power
Beauty trumps power or blood to trump power
Justice trumps power or blood to trump power
The names alive are like the names in the graves

AMERICAN SONNET FOR MY PAST AND FUTURE ASSASSIN

You don't seem to want it, but you wanted it.
You don't seem to want it, but you won't admit it.
You don't seem to want admittance.
You don't seem to want admission.
You don't seem to want it, but you haunt it.
You don't seem too haunted, but you haunted.
You don't seem to get it, but you got it.
You don't seem to care, but you care.
You don't seem to buy it, but you sell it.
You don't seem to want it, but you wanted it.
You don't seem to prey, but you prey,
You don't seem to pray but you full of prayers,
You don't seem to want it, but you wanted it.
You don't seem too haunted, but you haunted.

AMERICAN SONNET FOR MY PAST AND FUTURE ASSASSIN

Aryans, Betty Crocker, Bettye LaVette,
Blowfish, briar bushes, Bubbas, Buckras,
Archie Bunkers, bullhorns, bullwhips, bullets,
All cancers kill me, car crashes, cavemen, chakras,
Crackers, discord, dissonance, doves, Elvis,
Ghosts, the grim reaper herself, a heart attack
While making love, hangmen, Hillbillies exist,
Lillies, Martha Stewarts, Mayflower maniacs,
Money grubbers, Gwen Brooks' "The Mother,"
(My mother's bipolar as bacon), pancakes kill me,
Phonies, dead roaches, big roaches & smaller
Roaches, the sheepish, snakes, all seven seas,
Snow avalanches, swansongs, sciatica, Killer
Wasps, yee-haws, you, now & then, disease.

AMERICAN SONNET FOR MY PAST AND FUTURE ASSASSIN

Even the most kindhearted white woman,
Dragging herself through traffic with her nails
On the wheel & her head in a chamber of black
Modern American music may begin, almost
Carelessly, to breathe n-words. Yes, even the most
Bespectacled hallucination cruising the lanes
Of America may find her tongue curls inward,
Entangling her windpipe, her vents, toes & pedals
When she drives alone. Even the most made up
Layers of persona in a two- or four-door vehicle
Sealed in a fountain of bass & black boys
Chanting n-words may begin to chant inwardly
Softly before she can catch herself. Of course,
After that, what is inward, is absorbed.

AMERICAN SONNET FOR MY PAST AND FUTURE ASSASSIN

Seven of the ten things I love in the face
Of James Baldwin concern the spiritual
Elasticity of his expressions. The sashay
Between left & right eyebrow, for example.
The crease between his eyes like a tuning
Fork or furrow, like a riverbed branching
Into tributaries like lines of rapturous sentences
Searching for a period. The dimple in his chin
Narrows & expands like a pupil. Most of all,
I love all of his eyes. And those wrinkles
The feel & color of wet driftwood in the mud
Around those eyes. Mud is made of
Simple rain & earth, the same baptismal
Spills & hills of dirt James Baldwin is made of.

AMERICAN SONNET FOR MY PAST AND FUTURE ASSASSIN

The earth of my nigga eyes are assassinated.
The deep well of my nigga throat is assassinated.
The tender bells of my nigga testicles are gone.
You assassinate the sound of our bullshit & blissfulness.
The bones managing the body's business are cloaked
Until you assassinate my nigga flesh. The skin is replaced
By a cloak of fire. Sometimes it is river or rainwater
That cloaks the bones. Sometimes we lie on the roadside
In bushels of knotted roots, flowers & thorns until our body
Is found. You assassinate the smell of my breath, which is like
Smoke, milk, twilight itself. You assassinate my tongue
Which is like the head of a turtle wearing my skull for a shell.
You assassinate my lovely legs & the muscular hook of my cock.
Still, I speak for the dead. You will never assassinate my ghosts.

AMERICAN SONNET FOR MY PAST AND FUTURE ASSASSIN

I'm not sure how to hold my face when I dance:
In an expression of determination or euphoria?
And how should I look at my partner: in her eyes
Or at her body? Should I mirror the rhythm of her hips,
Or should I take the lead? I hear Jimi Hendrix
Was also unsure in dance despite being beautiful
And especially attuned. Most black people know this
About him. He understood the rhythm of a delta
Farmer on guitar in a juke joint circa 1933, as well
As the rhythm of your standard bohemian on guitar
In a New York apartment amid daydreams of jumping
Through windows, ballads of footwork, Monk orchestras,
Miles with strings. Whatever. I'm just saying,
I don't know how to hold myself when I dance. Do you?

AMERICAN SONNET FOR MY PAST AND FUTURE ASSASSIN

We suppose Ms. Dickinson is like the abandoned
Lover of Orpheus & too, that she loved to masturbate
Whispering lonely dark blue lullabies to Death.
Because Galway Kinnell writes of Saint Francis
Whose touch made a sow ecstatic, consider
How it would be to make every creature shudder
In orgasm. If you got one of your paws on a black-
Bird, you'd see the blackbird shift & shatter like
A vessel of ink. If you brushed the ear of a stranger,
Her jaw & eyes & fingers would clench on a dark
Blue feeling. If, like the bear in a deep image poem,
You got a paw on a fish in a river, you would feel
The fish convulse like the flesh flooded with blood
And the dark blue crush of touching yourself to Death.

AMERICAN SONNET FOR MY PAST AND FUTURE ASSASSIN

Probably, ghosts are allergic to us. Our uproarious
Breathing & ruckus. Our eruptions, our disregard
For dust. Small worlds unwhirl in the corners of our homes
After death. Our warriors, weirdos, antiheroes, our sirs,
Sires, our sighers, sidewinders & whiners, winos,
And wonders become dust. I know a few of the dead.
I remember my sister's last hoorah. I remember
The horror of her head on a pillow. For a long time
The numbers were balanced. The number alive equal
To the number in graves. After a very long time
The bones become dust again & the dust
After a long time becomes dirt & the dirt becomes soil
And the soil becomes grain again. This bitter earth is a song
Clogging the mouth before it is swallowed or spat out.

AMERICAN SONNET FOR MY PAST AND FUTURE ASSASSIN

Maxine Waters, being of fire, being of sword
Shaped like a silver tongue. Cauldron, siren,
Black as tarnation, black as the consciousness
Of a black president's wife, black as his black tie
Tuxedo beside his black wife in room after room
Of whiteness. My grandmother's name had water
In it too, Water maker. I have wept listening
To Aretha Franklin sing Precious Lord. I have placed
My thumb on the tongue of a black woman
With an unbreakable voice. I love your mouth,
Flood gate, storm door, you are black as the gap
In Baldwin's teeth, you are black as a Baldwin speech.
I love how your blackness leaves them in the dark.
I love how even your sound-bite leaves a mark.

AMERICAN SONNET FOR MY PAST AND FUTURE ASSASSIN

For her last birthday I found in a used New Jersey
Toy store, a six inch Amiri Baraka action figure
With three different outfits: an elaborately colored
Dashiki with afro pick; a black linen Leninist getup,
And a sports coat with elbow patches & wool Kangol.
Accessories include an ink pen & his father's pistol.
If you dip him in bathwater, he will leak
The names of his abandoned children. Pull a string,
He sings "Preface to a Twenty Volume Suicide Note"
Sweeter than the sweetest alto to ever sing
In the Boys Choir of Harlem. The store clerk tried
Selling me the actual twenty volume note LeRoi Jones
Wrote the night before Baraka put a bullet in him.
I would've bought it. But I had no room in my suitcase.

AMERICAN SONNET FOR MY PAST AND FUTURE ASSASSIN

A brother versed in ideological & material swagger
Seeks dime ass trill bitch starved enough to hang
Doo-ragged in smoke she can smell & therefore inhale
And therefore feel. Must ride shotgun pouring fountains
Of bass upon the landscape. Must be fat assed, fearless,
And God-fearing, an ancestral insurgent, clean
As new money, a cryptographer, a storyteller,
A glossy sleeve. There will be a jewelry of wooing.
There will be stacks of folded longing. Amid twilight
Verbiage in parking lots smelling of live wire, liquor
Hot air & fire: accompany a brother. Shout outs to vixens
And bitches out there twerking for fucks in Bluff Estates,
Washington Park, Star Light, Shop Road, Joe Frazier,
Harlem Street: this is daddy's boy. Who want it?

AMERICAN SONNET FOR MY PAST AND FUTURE ASSASSIN

But there never was a black male hysteria:
As if you weren't the spouse of Toni Morrison,
Forced by love to watch her flower, as well as
Literally expand. The locks of her hair prevented
Your skin from ever touching her skin. You never
Smelled the nape of her neck, though you glimpsed
It when her head cocked to illuminate paper. As if
Everything was a tool or weapon. Often you offered
Your measure, but she preferred her own song.
As if to make your blackness more strange,
More elaborate, more characteristic, fine-tuned
And refined. Soaphead Church, Empire State, Guitar,
Gideon, Son. The hysteria of being multiplied & divided
In your lover's mind until you go out of your mind.

AMERICAN SONNET FOR MY PAST AND FUTURE ASSASSIN

Our sermon today concerns the dialectic
Blessings in transgression & transcendence.
We're on the middle floor where the darkness
We bury is equal to the lightness we intend.
We stand in the valley & go to our knees
On the mountain. One rope pulls a body down
And into earth, the other pulls up & after stars.
To be divided is to be multiplied. Let us
Ponder how it is that you & I have remained
Alive. Mississippi & all the seas bound to sky by rain,
The root & reach of all the trees. When the wound
Is deep, the healing is heroic. Suffering and
Ascendance require the same work. Our sermon
Today sets the beauty of sin against the purity of dirt.

AMERICAN SONNET FOR MY PAST AND FUTURE ASSASSIN

Something in the metaphor of the bow
Which is never close enough to see the arrow
Hit its mark. I remain a mystery to my father.
My father remains a mystery to me.
Christianity is a religion built around a father
Who does not rescue his son. It is the story
Of a son whose father is a ghost. No one
Mentions Jesus' sister. Nothing is written
About her. She had no children, she was in her
Forties the first time she turned water into wine.
A late bloomer, she began a small wine business
And traveled all over the world selling the wine.
Her name was the name of the wine.
I don't recall the name of the wine.

AMERICAN SONNET FOR MY PAST AND FUTURE ASSASSIN

An old woman looks at the rows of clothes
She will never wear again. Beneath the clothes
Are high & low high heels, office & casual flats,
Sandals, & sneakers covered in dust while above
The rows of clothes is a shelf of tropic, exotic,
Cryptic, elegiac, futuristic Sunday hats amassed
Over many decades shopping wherever a woman
Buys such hats. The feathers stand like flags
In an overpopulated bird country where almost
Every export is covered or stuffed with feathers;
Where birds to survive disguise themselves as hats.
The old woman with a mess of feathers in her care
Is as lovely as she was long ago when she was known
To wear, every night, a different feather behind her ear.

AMERICAN SONNET FOR MY PAST AND FUTURE ASSASSIN

Maybe I was too hard on Derek Walcott.
In preschool while I lay on a nylon cot
In a church basement staring at God knows
What, I was not asleep when the old deacon
Snuck downstairs to let the two sisters
Watching over us lay hands against his advances.
His crown was haloed in gray, but eyebrows
And eyelashes swirled black as calligraphy
Around his gaze. "Cut it out," I'd hear the girl
With plump, plum lips say. He wore a silver
Bracelet, he spoke with a radiant sway,
Everywhere he was known to pray a prayer
So blood-filled & persuasive some listeners
Were said to fever, kneel, beg, break, levitate.

AMERICAN SONNET FOR MY PAST AND FUTURE ASSASSIN

On some level, I'm always full of Girl Scout cookies
In the land of a failed landlord with a people of color
Complex. On some level every action is an affirmation
Of personality. In the near empty subway car
I watched a brother dance on the ceiling, spin
On the subway pole like a stripper, twirl like an inverted
Ballerina on the parallel bars. I had no money
To give him. I was going to the party as Will Smith
In the first half of the *Hancock* movie: aloof, gifted,
Fucked up. I saw the shadows of planes gallop
Over buildings. I saw five white girls side by side
On a park bench, almost synchronized taking selfies
Of themselves taking selfies together in the land
Of a failed landlord with a people of color complex.

AMERICAN SONNET FOR MY PAST AND FUTURE ASSASSIN

America, you just wanted change is all, a return
To the kind of awe experienced after beholding a reign
Of gold. A leader whose metallic narcissism is a reflection
Of your own. You share a fantasy with Trinidad
James, who said, "Gold all in my chain, gold all in my ring,
Gold all in my watch" & if you know what I'm talking
About, your gold is the yellow of "Lemonade" by Gucci
Mane: "Yellow rims, yellow big booty, yellow bones,
Yellow Lambs, yellow MP's, yellow watch." Like no
Culture before us, we relate the way the descendants
Of the raped relate to the descendants of their rapists.
May your restlessness come at last to rest, constituents
Of Midas. I wish you the opposite of what Neruda said
Of lemons. May all the gold you touch burn, rot & rust.

AMERICAN SONNET FOR MY PAST AND FUTURE ASSASSIN

You know how when the light you splatter spreads
Across her back like wings tattooed elaborately one evening
In an ink-shop beside a river, how with the raw blood
Settling again into the meat you are you slump backwards
Half thinking it is more falling than slumping, more heartbreak
Than release & how maybe it's the wings that are real
Or that will become real when you are dust, Money,
When you have slipped again into the black husk
That is not a black husk at all? That's the feeling
Of her name in my mouth. It is like reaching a town
Bruised by headlights after too long in the darkness,
Like the feeling of one question flush against another,
The feeling of wings clasping the back of the body,
The feeling of wings clapping wind along the spine.

AMERICAN SONNET FOR MY PAST AND FUTURE ASSASSIN

If you have never felt what is fluid
In a woman run warm along your thighs
And testicles, Mister Trumpet if you do not know
The first man was in fact a woman whose clit
Grew so swollen with longing it hung like a finger
Pointing toward the lover stirring her meadows
Mister Trumpet what the fuck do you know
You are lonely because you could never unhitch
Your mother's terrifying radiant woe
I mean my mother here she the crazy bitch in me
She the way I weep she the way I break she manly
Trumpet I can't speak for you but men like me
Who have never made love to a man will always be
Somewhere in the folds of our longing ashamed of it

AMERICAN SONNET FOR MY PAST AND FUTURE ASSASSIN

Rilke ends his sonnet "Archaic Torso of Apollo" saying
"You must change your life." James Wright ends "Lying
In a Hammock at William Duffy's Farm in Pine Island,
Minnesota" saying "I have wasted my life." Ruth Stone ends
"A Moment" saying "You do not want to repeat my life."
A minute seed with a giant soul kicking inside it at the end
And beginning of life. After the opening scene where
A car bomb destroys the black detective's family, there are
Several scenes of our hero at the edge of life. A shootout
In an African American Folk Museum, a shootout
In the middle of an interstate rest stop parking lot,
A barn shootout endangering the farm life. I live a life
That burns a hole through life, that leaves a scar for life,
That makes me weep for another life. Define life.

AMERICAN SONNET FOR MY PAST AND FUTURE ASSASSIN

Goddamn, so this is what it means to have a leader
You despise, the racists said when the president
Was black and I'll be damned if I ain't saying it too.
Is this a mandate for whiteness, virility, sovereignty,
Stupidity, an idiot's threats & gangsta narcissisms threading
Every shabby sentence his trumpet constructs? You
Are not allowed to say shit about Mexicans when you
Ain't actually got any Mexican friends—I bet you've never
Been invited to a family dinner. You ain't allowed to deride
Women when you've never wept in front of a woman
That wasn't your mother. America's struggle with itself
Has always had people like me at the heart of it. You can't
Grasp your own hustle, your blackness, you can't grasp
Your own pussy, your black pussy dies for touch.

AMERICAN SONNET FOR MY PAST AND FUTURE ASSASSIN

Probably all our encounters are existential
Jambalaya. Which is to say, can a nigga survive?
Would you rather have happiness or freedom,
Pain or boredom? Would you rather hitch
Your rotten rope to a wagon or hitch your rotten
Wagon to a leash? After blackness was invented
People began seeing ghosts. When my father
Told me I was one of God's chosen ones,
He was only half bullshitting. Probably each twilight
Is as different as a father is from his son.
Something happens everywhere in this country
Every day. Someone is praying, someone is prey.
Probably blindness has a chewed heart
In its belly, or a gate opening upon another gate.

AMERICAN SONNET FOR MY PAST AND FUTURE ASSASSIN

I'm full of more water than a forest
And the adrenaline of a spooked horse.
But I'm a Time Lord. My armor is flesh
And spirit. I carry a flag bearing a different
Nation on each side. I carry money bearing
The face of my assassins. I'm good company
And pretty fun for a little while. A whirlwind,
I tend to repeat my mistakes. I'm a camera
With no cameraman, my own personal
Assistant & assassin. The truth is easy to see
When it's before you, but it's deceptive
Otherwise. I am selfish. I am a religion.
You are a religion. Together we are a religion.
My love is oppressive. I'm a Time Lord.

AMERICAN SONNET FOR MY PAST AND FUTURE ASSASSIN

But there never was a black male hysteria:
As if you weren't the lover of Langston Hughes,
Forced to hold what you knew of his measure
Secret until it drove you mad enough to cruise
The dive bars reciting the poems he wrote
About you but never published or spoke:
Lines covered in bruises & stars, almost
Unhinged lyrics. The man was high yellow
In public, afraid of himself, pretending his music
Was material when in fact, it was the opposite:
Like a breath that comes so quickly you know
You're breathing ether: either atmospheric
And anonymous as the air against a window,
Or indefinite & mute as a curtain of wind.

Because he cannot distinguish a blackbird
From a crow or raven, it's all the more
Brazen when the autocrat kisses a cat.
Because he's a kettle of oil about to boil,
It's all the more touching when the despot
Pets a pet. *The skin breaks so easily*, he says,
But he cries it softly. Because he's someone
Who can't distinguish a horse from a zebra
Without the stripes, he can't describe himself
Without looking in a mirror. Baller. Bawler.
Dentures. Makeup. He's almost too flakey
To be the villain. Because he's someone
Who cannot distinguish meat from malarkey.
Anything close to his mouth gets bitten.

AMERICAN SONNET FOR MY PAST AND FUTURE ASSASSIN

Sometimes the father almost sees looking
At the son, how handsome he'd be if half
His own face was made of the woman he loved.
He almost sees in his boy's face, an openness
Like a wound before it scars, who he was
Long before his name was lost, the trail
To his future on earth long before he arrived.
To be dead & alive at the same time.
A son finds his father handsome because
The son can almost see how he might
Become superb as the scar above a wound.
And because the son can see who he was
Long before he had a name, the trace of
His future on earth long before he arrived.

AMERICAN SONNET FOR MY PAST AND FUTURE ASSASSIN

It feels sadder when a black person says Nigga
Because it sounds like Nigger. It feels sadder
When a brother or sister says Nigga because
It sounds like Nigger. I have never heard either
Word in the mouth of my mother or father.
Once I had a lover who said neither word
Out loud. I used neither word for years.
It feels sadder to hear a nigga say Nigga when
It sounds like Nigger. Nothing saddens me more
Than Nigger, one whose master has no Lord.
No word leaves me more graced by shame.
You will always be my nigga, I say to the mirror
Because it is a dark water the temperature
Of a blade, the yellow flower stalking a dream.

AMERICAN SONNET FOR MY PAST AND FUTURE ASSASSIN

The subject is allowed up to twenty years
After leaving the home of his or her parents
To reconcile all but the darkest of infractions.
The deeper the wound the more heroic
The healing. As the story of Aeneas is *The Aeneid*
And the story of Odysseus, *The Odyssey*, the name
Of the subject is as mysterious as the journey.
The subject must speak as if he or she is witness
To a story no one who has lived in the entire
Tangled future & history of the world has told.
What if it were possible to make a noise so lovely
People would pay to hear it continuously for a century
Or so. Unbelievably, Miles Davis & John Coltrane
Standing within inches of each other didn't explode.

AMERICAN SONNET FOR MY PAST AND FUTURE ASSASSIN

The song must be cultural, confessional, clear
But not obvious. It must be full of compassion
And crows bowing in a vulture's shadow.
The song must have six sides to it & a clamor
Of voltas. The song must turn on the compass
Of language like a tangle of wire endowed
With feeling. The notes must tear & tear,
There must be a love for the minute & minute,
There must be a record of witness & daydream.
Where the heart is torn or feathered & tarred,
Where death is undone, time diminished,
The song must hold its own storm & drum,
And shed a noise so lovely it is sung at sunset
Weddings, baptisms & beheadings henceforth.

AMERICAN SONNET FOR MY PAST AND FUTURE ASSASSIN

A remix of "Pony" by Ginuwine plays
While half a dozen beautiful black men
Strut onstage wearing translucent black
Housecoats then pause with their backs
To us before a slow twerking as half a dozen
Beautiful black women walk onstage in sharp
Alabaster tuxedoes and surgical masks
But we can see the weeping inside them.
A white audience member, it may be a man
Or woman of any age, is invited up to crow
In the middle of a circle the dancers make.
I have sent tickets of this show to my white friend
Who is determined to write about black people
And to my black friends determined to police him.

The umpteenth thump on the rump of a badunkadunk
Stumps us. The lunk, the chump, the hunk of plunder.
The umpteenth horny, honky stump speech pumps
A funky rumble over air. The umpteenth slump
In our humming democracy, a bumble bureaucracy
With teeny tiny wings too small for its rumpled,
Dumpling of a body. Humpty-Dumpy. Frumpy
Suit. The umpteenth honk of hollow thunder.
The umpteenth *Believe me.* The umpteenth grumpy,
Jumpy retort. Chump change, casino game, tuxedo,
Teeth bleach, stump speech. Junk science. Junk bond.
Junk country, stump speech. The umpteenth boast
Stumps our toe. The umpteenth falsehood stumps
Our elbows & eyeballs, our Nos, Whoahs, wows, woes.

AMERICAN SONNET FOR MY PAST AND FUTURE ASSASSIN

Drive like fifteen miles along a national parkway
Where the confederate statues have been painted
White so often they will probably look like ghosts
Or men covered in sheets at the speed you pass them.
Join the bottleneck at the mouth of the tunnel running
Beneath fathoms of the river. You may recall a bomb
Was set off there some years ago: Caution tape,
A rise in cargo takes, a till of bodies bobbed at the piers.
How much have black people been paid for naming
Emmett Till in poems? How much is owed? Never mind.
Never fear, the tunnel under the uproarious river
Around our lives has been repaired. When you exit,
Take the second right toward the oldest part of town,
You will find me bearing a sign on one of the corners there.

AMERICAN SONNET FOR MY PAST AND FUTURE ASSASSIN

After you turn off Shop Road where the flag leans
Forward like an old goose contemplating her next step,
Ride for another half hour or so beyond Bluff Estates,
Star Light & Harlem Street to find inside
What is Betty Joe's Fish & Chicken Shack by day,
A mobilized after hours juke joint full of the kinds
Of dancers & drinkers, loners & lovers who have
Probably never listened to a poem or banjo at length.
In this we may be alike, Assassin, you & me: we believe
We want what's best for humanity. I'll probably survive
Dancing with the kinds of people who must find refuge
Among the sweat & rancor of a Fish & Chicken Shack
But Assassin, they'll probably murder you. Do you ask,
Why you should die for me if I will not die for you? I do.

AMERICAN SONNET FOR MY PAST AND FUTURE ASSASSIN

This one goes out to DeMascas Jackson,
Who named his beloved pit bull "DeMarcus"
Because he wanted a twin & named each part
Of his body, "nigga": his ten dirty danglers,
His fifteen-year-old bully elbows & regions
Of his mouth running between lunch & bells.
"I bit that nigga," he said once of his bitten lip
Over cafeteria hair in a salad of withered lettuce
And shaved carrots. When I called him "DeMarcus"
In the heat of a game, "That's my nigga," he said
Before shoving me into the same fence I'd stand at
An hour later holding my father's crippled pistol,
With no bullets & no wooden handgrip, so I held
A little frame of metal in my fist when I pointed it.

AMERICAN SONNET FOR MY PAST AND FUTURE ASSASSIN

Because a law was passed that said there was no worth
To adjectives, companies began stringing superlatives
Before unchanged products manufactured by men
Who know how to make money, but nothing else.
After a law was passed that said there was no worth
To adjectives, the afflicted became addicted to property.
Because they passed a law that said there was no worth
To adjectives, all the news was as bilateral as a headline
In the sand. A racehorse became a horse, a horse race
Became a race. The race was made of various adverbs
And adversaries. The relationship between future
And pasture was lost. Because a law was passed,
There was no worth to adjectives, there was no word
For the part of the pasture between departure & the past.

AMERICAN SONNET FOR MY PAST AND FUTURE ASSASSIN

But there never was a black male hysteria
Breaking & entering wearing glee & sadness
And the light grazing my teeth with my lighter
To the night with the flame like a blade cutting
Me slack along the corridors with doors of offices
Orifices vomiting tears & fire with my two tongues
Loose & shooing under a high top of language
In a layer of mischief so traumatized trauma
Delighted me beneath the tremendous
Stupendous horrendous undiscovered stars
Burning where I didn't know how to live
My friends were all the wounded people
The black girls who held their own hands
Even the white boys who grew into assassins

AMERICAN SONNET FOR MY PAST AND FUTURE ASSASSIN

Any day now you will have the ability to feed the name
Of anyone into an engine & your long lost half brother
As well as whoever else possesses a version of his name
Will appear before your face in bits of pixels & data
Displaying his monikers (like Gitmo for trapping, Bang
Bang for banging, Dopamine for dope or brains),
The country he would most like to visit (Heaven),
His nine & middle finger pointing towards the arms
Of the last trill trees of Bluff Estates & the arms
Of the slim fly girls the color of trees cut down & shaped
Into something a nail penetrates. I admit, right now:
Technology is insufficient, but you will find them
Flashing grins & money in the photos they took
Before they were ghosts when you click here tomorrow.

AMERICAN SONNET FOR MY PAST AND FUTURE ASSASSIN

This word can be the difference between knowing
And thinking. It's the name people of color call
Themselves on weekends & the name colorful
People call their enemies & friends. It used to be
The word for the absence of inheritance. Before that
It was the word for the feel of burlap. When Lincoln
Witnessed a slave auction in his boyhood, it was
The first word to enter his mind. Before it evoked
A kind of bewildering mothering, it evoked Job's
Afro silvering with suffering. It is the difference
Between cursive, tantrum, assault & pepper spray.
It is the title of that absurd three-act play
Where the actors say nothing but "Who can say"
And who can say "Who can say" for two hours straight.

AMERICAN SONNET FOR MY PAST AND FUTURE ASSASSIN

Why someone would crowd into a church is beyond me.
I would remodel Alabama. Why there is a science
For God is beyond me the way the word *wallop*
Is beyond me. And when my id is arrested, I am usually
Thinking of the tragi-comic implications of the word
Mall & eyeballing midriffs. Why youth seems to be
My only requisite for beauty now is beyond me.
The interiors of the words *botox* & *toy box* are beyond me too.
History is beyond me. I will need a black suit & umbrella now.
The carpet along the aisles will be so thick, our shoes
Will never touch the floor. Limousines tinted with flowers
Will be parked in front of the church. Ma will say "Good God,
Good God," dipping money in her eyes. But why
Give God your money? Why give good money to Death?

AMERICAN SONNET FOR MY PAST AND FUTURE ASSASSIN

From now on I will do my laundry early Sunday
Mornings when all the young tenants are hung-
Over or worn out, all the old people in church,
And the elementary parents parked at playgrounds
With their children inside the "Play At Your Own
Risk" sign on the fence. I tried to tell the woman
Who sent me songs, it's departure that makes company
Hard to master. I tried to tell her I'm a muser, a miser
With time. I love poems more than money & pussy.
From now on I will eat brunch alone. I believe
Eurydice is actually the poet, not Orpheus. Her muse
Has his back to her with his ear bent to his own heart.
As if what you learn making love to yourself matters
More than what you learn when loving someone else.

AMERICAN SONNET FOR MY PAST AND FUTURE ASSASSIN

Otherwise home is the mess laid bare,
The less made air, the addressless there
Less clear, where the wax in my left ear makes
Half of what's said unsaid, on the air the mute
Newshounds ponder the tweets of a bullhorn,
A rat in the cabinet beside the liquor. Anger
Is a form of heartbreak, yes it is. If you can
Give the world half of what Nina Simone gave it,
You will have lived an exceptional life. All you
Have to say is, tomorrow you'll try to be better.
Like a mother lovingly calling her son, a son
Of a bitch. My lover never believed I held a gun
In my mouth. So I talk to myself like a witness.
I'd mutter *whatever, whatever* forever otherwise.

AMERICAN SONNET FOR MY PAST AND FUTURE ASSASSIN

I thought we might as well sing the fables of sea
To fill our mouths before sailing out to whale.
I thought we might sing as well of the feeling
Of sea moving about the whale like a coat.
The color of water is always the temperature
Of a mirror. I thought we might drown
Our reflections in a swaying like our songs
Of mother wit & mother woe, our toasts
With the water a deep dark blue, an almost
Indigo we paled from the well before sail.
Whale-road is a kenning for sea. Time-machine
Is a kenning for the mind. Alive is a kenning
For the electrified. I thought we might sing
Of the wire wound round the wound of feeling.

AMERICAN SONNET FOR MY PAST AND FUTURE ASSASSIN

I'd played *silence* but later realized my word
Of the year was *quiet*. Especially the chasm
Of quiet in *cataclysm*, one of those scrabble words
Played but once or twice in a life. Maybe scrabble
Is a portmanteau of *scream* & *babble* or *scrap*
And *bramble*. Sometimes it is best to sting,
Sometimes it's better to scramble away. *Sometimes*
Is a good answer to any existential question.
Moving through the tangle of bramble on your way
To scrap with Death at the pier, remember to sing
A battle song. The one I've prepared goes this way:
Come & meet me in the water, swim the twilight by & by.
Come meet me in the water, swim the mirror of the skies
Come & meet me in the water by & by. I sing it every day.

AMERICAN SONNET FOR MY PAST AND FUTURE ASSASSIN

Suppose you could speak nothing but money
And acrimony. Suppose all the sunflowers
Van Gogh destroyed, all the stones in Virginia's
Pockets & all the stones Georgia painted as vaginas
Were simply a matter of making something greater
Than money. Prince taught us a real man has
A beautiful woman in him. Suppose we cannot
Forget what happened in Money. Suppose
You're someone who celebrates Thomas Jefferson's
Birthday. Suppose he was someone whose love
For a black woman was blinded by blackness,
Hers & his, yours & mine. I ain't mad at you,
Assassin. It's not the bad people who are brave
I fear, it's the good people who are afraid.

AMERICAN SONNET FOR MY PAST AND FUTURE ASSASSIN

One of the most amazing things about me is
I know how to cut my own hair. I learned to do it
After my father moved away. So I've done it
For years, traced the shape of my thinking
With a motor blade to rewrite the hairline
A punctuated sentence, a handful of verbiage,
I could offer a poem for each clippered hair
And the mole behind my ear & the line I fear
Above my nape, the rope burn there, the wish
To snip the jugular is simple fear, I wish to remain
Here where you will love me simply because
Of what I say: one of the most amazing things
About me is: I know how to cut my own hair.
I learned to do it after my father moved away.

AMERICAN SONNET FOR MY PAST AND FUTURE ASSASSIN

My mother says I am beautiful inside
And out. But my lover never believed it.
My lover never believed I held her name
In my mouth. My mother calls me her silver
Bullet. Her mercy pill, the metal along her spine.
I am my mother's bewildered shadow.
My lover's bewildering shadow is mine.
I have wept listening to a terrible bewildering
Music break over & through & break down
A black woman's voice. I talk to myself
Like her sister. Assassin, you are a mystery
To me, I say to my reflection sometimes.
You are beautiful because of your sadness, but
You would be more beautiful without your fear.

AMERICAN SONNET FOR MY PAST AND FUTURE ASSASSIN

A brother versed in spiritual calisthenics
And cowboy quiet seeks funny, lonesome,
Speculative or eye-glassed lass. Shopaholics
Welcomed. Also Prince fanatics, museum
Cashiers, & pragmatists conversant (lipstick
Or no lipstick) with a hipness substantial
Enough to contract around a muscle as well
As expand around a child. Fear of boredom is ideal.
Fear of dereliction is okay. Love for the willy-nilly
And Willie Nelson, welcomed. Crushes, depressions,
And unsightly hesitations are okay. Must freely
Expend humor & grace. Amid long Sundays,
Long drives, long movies, & school conferences,
Occasional acts of disregard or guardedness are okay.

AMERICAN SONNET FOR MY PAST AND FUTURE ASSASSIN

Glad someone shot deserved to be shot finally,
George Wallace. After you send your basket of balms
And berries for the girls the bomb buried in Birmingham,
After you add your palms to the psalms & palm covered
Caskets of the girls the bomb buried in Birmingham,
I'll muster a pinch of prayer for you. You are the blind
Protagonist of a story that begins, "In my previous life
My work involved returning runaway slaves to slavery,"
And ends with the image of a black nurse pushing
Your old ass in a wheelchair. Can you guess what black
Folk passing empty cotton fields feel, George Wallace?
I damn you with the opposite of that feeling. I keep thinking
I'm confessing for the first time, the reason I fear you,
And you keep asking why I'm telling this old story again.

AMERICAN SONNET FOR MY PAST AND FUTURE ASSASSIN

You have a gun but to use the bullet
You decide your wife, having snuggled it
Under her tongue, should then smuggle it
Into your pie hole but she swallows it.
You have a gun but to use the poison
You have your son dip a rose in venom
So strong the smell alone will kill someone,
But the first to die smelling it is your son.
You have a gun but to use the dagger
You decide your daughter should dangle
It beneath her dress. She refuses to endanger
Her self-respect. You need to find goons,
Wranglers, wire, gin, ingenuity, cotton gins,
You need the constitution. You have a gun.

AMERICAN SONNET FOR MY PAST AND FUTURE ASSASSIN

When I am nowhere near a ledge or knife covered
In a corridor of fever colored carpet or catching rain
Bead upon the morning headlights hungering some crash
To crack & blacken me before a train full of women
With nose rings & thigh boots, the curved ass of a mother
With her toddler & the rain still following the hills
And shoulders of parts of Maryland & New Jersey,
And the oncoming trains passing inches from head-on
Headlong into Newark where I almost escaped this path,
Before remembering the thrill coloring even today's
Melancholy delay asleep, awake, the wild haired woman
Smiling on the stairs before fading, a song in the ear
Like the broken phone booth I passed in the Village
Beside a puddle of what could have been crushed tomatoes

AMERICAN SONNET FOR MY PAST AND FUTURE ASSASSIN

I cut myself on some glass in the water.
I was out driving around the stars.
I was chopping wood out back.
I was at the abattoir grabbing a snack.
I was grabbing my phone in the truck.
I was smoking below the boat deck.
I was practicing electric guitar.
I was listening to aspiring laughter.
I was on the toilet with a magazine.
I was home awaiting a limousine.
I was bargaining with the mortician.
I was laying a great foundation.
I was practicing trumpet while drowning.
I was grinding my hooves to nails.

AMERICAN SONNET FOR MY PAST AND FUTURE ASSASSIN

When MLK was shot his blood changed to change
Wherever it hit the floor. Like the others,
Jackson & Abernathy gathered a few of the coins
For themselves. A few sank into the pockets
Of the detectives & forensic scientists, reporters.
A maid sold the penny she found for a pretty penny
On the black market. It is in a display case beside
The bullets Du Bois kept in the gun under his bed.
Bird got so high on horn, he disappeared. X grew
Large as a three hundred year old tree colonizing
The landscape. In the game of "chicken" two drivers
Speed towards each other & if the one who is chicken
Does not swerve, both drivers may die in the crash.
This country is mine as much as an orphan's house is his.

AMERICAN SONNET FOR MY PAST AND FUTURE ASSASSIN

Later the white boy we once beat like a drum
Died after crashing his Camaro around a bend
Off Shop Road. He was an asshole. Ask the baby
Black boys he bullied at Robert E. Lee Middle School
Where the Robert E. Lee statue was painted white
So often over the years it looked like someone
Covered in a sheet of glue. I would not have liked
To attend a middle school named after Emmett Till
Or for that matter, any murdered black person.
When I was the age of Emmett Till, I reckoned
MLK was an old man at the age he was killed.
I am old enough now to know the drum, though beaten,
Is not an instrument of violence. Nor is a banjo
Or whistle. I'm sorry I missed the white boy's funeral.

AMERICAN SONNET FOR MY PAST AND FUTURE ASSASSIN

It was discovered the best way to combat
Sadness was to make your sadness a door.
Or make it an envelope of wireless chatter
Or wires pulled from the radio tape recorder
Your mother bought you for Christmas in 1984.
If you think a hammer is the only way to hammer
A nail, you ain't thought of the nail correctly.
My problem was I'd decided to make myself
A poem. It made me sweat in private selfishly.
It made me bleed, bleep & weep for health.
As a poem I could show my children the man
I dreamed I was, my mother & fathers, my half
Brothers, the lovers I lost. Just morning, as a poem,
I asked myself if I was going to weep today.

AMERICAN SONNET FOR MY PAST AND FUTURE ASSASSIN

But there never was a black male hysteria:
As if being called *Nigger* never makes you
Disappear. As if the fear of other people
Never makes you levitate. As if the nuzzle
Of a bullet can't poke a hole in your breath.
As if you cannot drink from the river
When into the river you disappear & water
Floods the hole in your breath. You make shit,
You piss, you calculate mistakes, you can turn
Stone into metal, you are able to breathe wind. Air
Touches your skin like medicine & you disappear.
It's crazy. It's as if you are not being hunted
By hysteria. It's as if your death is never death.
You appear, you appear to disappear, you disappear.

AMERICAN SONNET FOR MY PAST AND FUTURE ASSASSIN

In a parallel world where all Dr. Who's
Are black, I'm the doctor who knows no god
Is more powerful than Time. In a parallel world
Where all the doctors who are black see cops
Box black boys in cop cars & caskets, I'm
The doctor who blacks out whenever he sees
A police box. In a parallel world where doctors
Who box cops in caskets cry doing their jobs,
I disappear inside a skull that's larger on the inside.
Question: if, in a parallel world where every Dr.
Who was black, you were the complex Time Lord,
When & where would you explore? My answer is,
A brother has to know how to time travel & doctor
Himself when a knee or shoe stalls against his neck.

AMERICAN SONNET FOR MY PAST AND FUTURE ASSASSIN

Over-aged, over grave, overlooked brother
Seeks adjoining variable female structure
Covered in chocolate, cinnamon, molasses,
Freckled, sandy or sunset colored flesh
Expressively motored by a blend of intellectual
Fat & muscle while several complex & simple
Emotional frequencies pulse along her veins.
Must be a careful & moderately self-indulgent
Cinematographer, modestly self-conscious, reasonably
Self-important, spiritually self-educated, marginally
Self-destructive. Must be willing to raise orchids
Or kids in a land of assassins; willing to wield a fluid
Expression in the war her lover wages against himself,
And a silver tongue in the war we wage against death.

AMERICAN SONNET FOR MY PAST AND FUTURE ASSASSIN

I only intend to send word to my future
Self perpetuation is a war against Time
Travel is essentially the aim of any religion
Is blindness the color one sees under water
Breath can be overshadowed in darkness
The benefits of blackness can seem radical
Black people in America are rarely compulsive
Hi-fivers believe joy is a matter of touching others
Is forbidden the only word God doesn't know
You have to heal yourself to truly be heroic
You have to think once a day of killing your self
Awareness requires a touch of blindness & self
Importance is the only word God knows
To be free is to live because only the dead are slaves

AMERICAN SONNET FOR MY PAST AND FUTURE ASSASSIN

In the saddest part of the story the brother says
To the muse of his heartache, Don't you ever
Come near my grave. The saddest scene is where
The daughter's ghost says to the mother, Don't
Come near my grave. The frail speckled shell says
To the shy yolk it meant to protect, but only held
Captive, Don't you ever come near my grave.
The saddest part of the opera is where Frida says it
To Diego. The saddest moment is where the gifted
Says it to the gift giver & the moment where
The present says it to yesterday: you have to love me
Better. The moment where the prisoner says it
To the future & the pastor. The saddest part is where
The dirt says it to the seeds in the flowers above the grave.

AMERICAN SONNET FOR MY PAST AND FUTURE ASSASSIN

I remember my sister's last hoorah.
She joined all the black people I'm tired of losing,
All the dead from parts of Florida, Ferguson,
Brooklyn, Charleston, Cleveland, Chicago,
Baltimore, wherever the names alive are
Like the names in graves. I am someone
With a good memory & better imagination.
Can we really be friends if we don't believe
In the same things, Assassin? Probably,
Ghosts are allergic to us. Because we are dust,
Don't you & I share a loss, don't we belong
Together, Brother, Sweetness, Sweetness,
Sweetness? Poor, ragged Heart, blind, savage
Heart, I've almost grown tired of talking to you.

AMERICAN SONNET FOR MY PAST AND FUTURE ASSASSIN

When I am close enough, I am reminded
Of the mythic orchid called Lorca's Breath.
Named by Salvador Dalí a decade after the poet
Was killed, the flower is said to sprout petals
The shade of a swollen moon but once or twice
Before it dies. Also lost was the painting
Dalí painted of Lorca's writing hand: a long
Almost animal shadow crawling over land shaped
Like a man with the body of a woman. A cuff
Of celestial texture. A button of ruby. The orchid's
Mouth is the shade of pussy, its leaves hang
As if listening to a lover whisper with her back
To you. Rumor that this flower first appeared
Near wherever Lorca is buried, I know to be untrue.

Sonnet Index

ACKNOWLEDGMENTS

My gratitude for the support of the following journals: *The American Poetry Review, Baffler, Boston Review, Harvard Review, Indiana Review* (Ink Lit), *Kenyon Review, Literary Hub* (http://lithub.com/tag/poems/), *New England Review, The New Republic, The New Yorker, Ploughshares,* Poem-a-Day (April 25, 2017, www.poets.org/poetsorg/poem/american-sonnet-my-past-and-future-assassin), *Poetry, A Poetry Congeries,* and *Tin House.*

My gratitude for the support of the following institutions: the University of Pittsburgh, New York University, and the John D. and Catherine T. MacArthur Foundation.

I can't begin to account for all the love and friendship that made these poems possible. I made you a book of poems. A special career-enabling thank-you to Paul Slovak.

Many years ago the poet Anthony Butts told me he was writing a book called *Male Hysteria.* I loved the title and its many possibilities. Alas, the book never came to be. Maybe I'm not even remembering the title correctly. Still think of you, Brother.

These poems owe tremendous gratitude to the great Wanda Coleman (1946–2013). When asked in an interview with Paul E. Nelson how she'd give an assignment for writing an American Sonnet she said:

> First I would explain my process. Then I would invite my students to try
> it, overlaying their specific 1) issues (what the sonnet is about) 2) rhythms
> (places and devices often have them) 3) tones (shadings of attitude)
> 4) musical taste/preference (rock, classical, blues, etc.)—how to develop
> the minimal language to simultaneously encapsulate and signal each.

When asked for a definition she called the poems jazz sonnets "with certain properties—progression, improvisation, mimicry, etc." and concluded, "I decided to have fun—to blow my soul." American Sonnets Interview with Wanda Coleman—Global Voices Radio, Paul E. Nelson. www.globalvoices radio.org/American_Sonnets_Wanda_interview.

TERRANCE HAYES is the author of *Lighthead*, winner of the 2010 National Book Award and finalist for the National Book Critics Circle Award. His other books are *Wind in a Box*, *Hip Logic*, and *Muscular Music*. His honors include a National Endowment for the Arts Fellowship, a Guggenheim Fellowship, and a 2014 MacArthur Fellowship. *How to Be Drawn*, his most recent collection of poems, was a finalist for the 2015 National Book Award and received the 2016 NAACP Image Award for Poetry.

How to Be Drawn

A finalist for the National Book Award and the
National Book Critics Circle Award

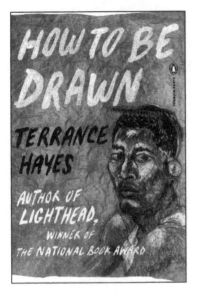

How is the self drawn by and to the paradoxes of the mind, body, and soul? How do we resist being withdrawn, erased? In his daring fifth collection, Terrance Hayes explores how we see and are seen. Simultaneously complex and transparent, urgent and composed, How to Be Drawn is a mesmerizing achievement.

"[His] poems are like a Pixar version of the mental marionette show, a dazzling space crammed with comic jabs."
—Dan Chiasson, The New Yorker

 PENGUIN BOOKS

Ready to find your next great read? Let us help. Visit prh.com/nextread

Lighthead

Winner of the National Book Award for Poetry

In his fourth collection, Terrance Hayes investigates how we construct experience. With one foot firmly grounded in the everyday and the other hovering in the air, his poems braid dream and reality into a poetry that is both dark and buoyant. Fueled by an imagination that enlightens, delights, and ignites, *Lighthead* leaves us illuminated and scorched.

"*Lighthead* displays a riffing, wildly relentless insistence and astonishing brio. . . .
Hayes breaks down categories and builds up forms with acrobatic glee."
–Megan O'Rourke, The Year's Best Poetry, NPR.org

Ⓟ PENGUIN BOOKS

Wind in a Box

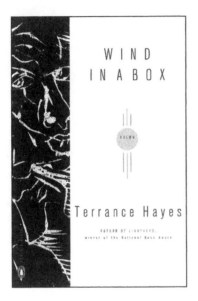

Through persona poems, prose poems, list poems, and lyric narratives, *Wind in a Box* examines change within order, freedom within containment, exploring how influence and tradition can be simultaneously upended and embraced. These poems look at how identity is both shaped and shrouded by culture; how the imagination is both enlarged and restricted by form.

"A distinctively American voice to take on the new complexities of race and the old hardships incumbent in being human. Hayes will disturb the comfortable and comfort the disturbed." —Mary Karr

 PENGUIN BOOKS

Ready to find your next great read? Let us help. Visit prh.com/nextread

Hip Logic

Winner of the National Poetry Series competition

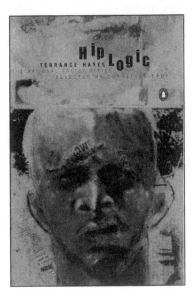

In *Hip Logic*, Terrance Hayes's verse dances in a kind of home-made music box, with notes that range from tender to erudite, associative to narrative, humorous to political. Full of poetic tributes to the likes of Paul Robeson, Big Bird, Balthus, and Mr. T, this dazzling collection confirms Hayes's reputation as a truly original writer and one of the most compelling voices in American poetry.

"Hayes is one elegant poet. First you'll marvel at his skill, his near-perfect pitch, his disarming humor, his brilliant turns of phrase. Then you'll notice the grace, the tenderness." —Cornelius Eady

 PENGUIN BOOKS